THE VOICES

& Other Poems

THE VOICES
& Other Poems

RAINER MARIA RILKE

Translated and with an introduction by
Kristofor Minta

ISBN 978-1-7349766-6-3
LCCN 2020948086

Manufactured in the United States of America
Printed on acid-free paper
Design and typesetting by Joshua Rothes

Seattle, WA, USA

SUBLUNARY
EDITIONS

Contents

Introduction

These poems do not contain much of the Rilke some of us are used to, the Rilke Auden called "the Santa Claus of loneliness". He's there, lingering at the entrance, but across the threshold steps a harder Rilke, and we must account for the anomaly this represents in his work. If a general impression of Rilke persists, one of subtle feeling, melancholy, and loneliness—it is partly because he promoted this version of himself. Ever conscious of self-image, even on his tombstone Rilke hands us a rose.

Yet the work here is different; it seems to care less about managing our perception than it does about piercing to the heart of things. Rilke appears to have found a freedom in leaving himself. In these poems, he adopts personae who genuinely own their lives, lives other than Rilke's—yet their voices remain unmistakably his work. Part of the pleasure in these pages, then, comes from feeling that the Rilke familiar to us has been made strange... and not knowing if we are quite as safe in his hands as we had previously assumed.

If narcissism is one of the hazards of the poet's trade, this slim volume proves that Rilke was aware of his faults in this regard. Addressing them, his poetry rose to new heights. These persona poems were, for the most part, developed concurrently with his celebrated *dinggedichte* (thing-poems) and were certainly part of the breakthrough that led to his mature work. And, though not often considered as such, Rilke's works in persona *are* thing-poems of a kind—subject-poems instead of object-poems—and equal in achievement to those better-known pieces. If we laud Rilke for showing us the inner life of a panther or a statue, then when he gives us the interior of a drunkard or a prisoner—or portrays the strange life that inheres in a corpse—we should offer equal praise.

—Kristofor Minta
August, 2020

Acknowledgements

Thanks to Florence Minta, Kat Robinson, Joshua Beckman, Michael Burkard, Joseph Fridlund, Joshua Rothes, Jessica Hurst, and Kirston Johnson.

Special thanks to Herbert Pföstl for his friendship, proofreading, and suggestions.

The present translation of "Eingang/Entrance" previously appeared in the 2017 supplement to the journal *Reliquae*.

Although one strives to escape one's self
as if trapped in some loathsome pit,
it is actually one of the world's great wonders:
I sense it: *all life will be lived.*
Who lives it, then?

from *The Book of Hours*

from **THE BOOK OF IMAGES**

Eingang

Wer du auch seist: am Abend tritt hinaus
aus deiner Stube, drin du alles weißt;
als letztes vor der Ferne liegt dein Haus:
wer du auch seist.

Mit deinen Augen, welche müde kaum
von der verbrauchten Schwelle sich befrein,
hebst du ganz langsam einen schwarzen Baum
und stellst ihn vor den Himmel: schlank, allein.
Und hast die Welt gemacht. Und sie ist groß

und wie ein Wort, das noch im Schweigen reift.
Und wie dein Wille ihren Sinn begreift,
lassen sie deine Augen zärtlich los...

Entrance

Whoever you are: in the evening step out
of your room, where everything's familiar;
your house lies between you and the distance:
whoever you are.

With your eyes, which are almost too weary
to free from the worn-out doorstep,
raise one black tree very slowly
and stand it before the heavens: slender, alone.
And you've made the world. And it is vast

and like a word which ripens even in silence.
And as your will grasps its meaning,
let your eyes gently leave it...

5

Die Braut

Ruf mich, Geliebter, ruf mich laut!
Laß deine Braut nicht so lange am Fenster Stehn.
In den alten Platanenalleen
wacht der Abend nicht mehr:
sie sind leer.

Und kommst du mich nicht in das nächtliche Haus
mit deiner Stimme verschließen,
so muß ich mich aus meinen Händen hinaus
in die Gärten des Dunkelblaus
ergießen...

The Bride

Call for me, my love, call loudly!
Don't let your bride wait so long by the window.
Evening no longer wakes
the old tree-lined avenues:
They are empty.

And if you won't come to me in the unlit house
you sealed with your voice,
then I must pour myself out of my own hands
into the dark blue gardens...

THE VOICES

Nine Leaves with a Title Leaf

Titelblatt

Die Reichen und Glücklichen haben gut schweigen,
niemand will wissen, was sie sind.
Aber die Dürftigen müssen sich zeigen,
müssen sagen: ich bin blind,
oder: ich bin im Begriff es zu werden
oder: es geht mir nicht gut auf Erden,
oder: ich habe ein krankes Kind,
oder: da bin ich zusammengefügt ...

Und vielleicht, daß das gar nicht genügt.

Und weil alle sonst, wie an Dingen,
an ihnen vorbeigehn, müssen sie singen.

Und da hört man noch guten Gesang.

Freilich die Menschen sind seltsam; sie hören
lieber Kastraten in Knabenchören.

Aber Gott selber kommt und bleibt lang,
wenn ihn diese Beschnittenen stören.

Title Leaf

The rich and happy had best keep quiet,
no one wants to know what they are.
But the destitute must exhibit themselves,
must say: I am blind
or: it won't be long until I am
or: nothing on earth goes goes my way
or: I have a sick child
or: here is where I'm stitched together...

And perhaps, even that isn't enough.

And because they get passed by
like objects otherwise, they must sing.

And that's where you can still hear good singing.

People certainly are strange; they'd rather
hear castrati in boy's choirs.

But God himself looks in and even lingers
when *these* scarred ones sing out.

Das Lied des Bettlers

Ich gehe immer von Tor zu Tor,
verregnet und verbrannt;
auf einmal leg ich mein rechtes Ohr
in meine rechte Hand.
Dann kommt mir meine Stimme vor,
als hätt ich sie nie gekannt.

Dann weiß ich nicht sicher, wer da schreit,
ich oder irgendwer.
Ich schreie um eine Kleinigkeit.
Die Dichter schrein um mehr.

Und endlich mach ich noch mein Gesicht
mit beiden Augen zu;
wie's dann in der Hand liegt mit seinem Gewicht,
sieht es fast aus wie Ruh.
Damit sie nicht meinen, ich hätte nicht,
wohin ich mein Haupt tu.

The Song of the Beggar

I go from door to door forever,
rained on and sunburnt;
suddenly I put my right ear
in my right hand.
Then my voice seems
as if I had never heard it before.

Then I can't be sure who is yelling,
me or someone else.
I shout over a trifle.
Less even than what poets shout about.

And in the end, I make a face
with both eyes closed;
how it lies then, with its weight in my hand,
almost looks like rest.
Lest they think I had no place
to lay my head.

Das Lied des Blinden

Ich bin blind, ihr draußen, das ist ein Fluch,
ein Widerwillen, ein Widerspruch,
etwas täglich Schweres.
Ich leg meine Hand auf den Arm der Frau,
meine graue Hand auf ihr graues Grau,
und sie führt mich durch lauter Leeres.
Ihr rührt euch und rückt und bildet euch ein,
anders zu klingen als Stein auf Stein,
aber ihr irrt euch: ich allein
lebe und leide und lärme.
In mir ist ein endloses Schrein,
und ich weiß nicht, schreit mir mein
Herz oder meine Gedärme.
Erkennt ihr die Lieder? Ihr sanget sie nicht,
nicht ganz in dieser Betonung.
Euch kommt jeden Morgen das neue Licht
warm in die offene Wohnung.
Und ihr habt ein Gefühl von Gesicht zu Gesicht,
und das verleitet zur Schonung.

The Song of the Blind Man

I am blind, you out there. It's a curse,
a reluctance, a contradiction,
heavy every day.
I place my hand on the woman's arm,
my gray hand on her grayish gray,
and she leads me through sheer emptiness.

You agitate and bump about and suppose that you
ring differently than stone on stone,
but you err: I alone
live and suffer and swear.
In me is an endless howl
and I don't know if it's my heart
that cries or my bowels.

Recognize the songs? You don't sing them-
not quite with this weight.
Every morning the new light arrives
warm into your welcoming home.
And you have a face to face feeling
that tempts you toward mercy.

Das Lied des Trinkers

Es war nicht in mir. Es ging aus und ein.
Da wollt ich es halten. Da hielt es der Wein.
(Ich weiß nicht mehr, was es war.)
Dann hielt er mir jenes und hielt mir dies,
bis ich mich ganz auf ihn verließ.
Ich Narr.
Jetzt bin ich in seinem Spiel, und er streut
mich verächtlich herum und verliert mich noch heut
an dieses Vieh, an den Tod.
Wenn der mich, schmutzige Karte, gewinnt,
so kratzt er mit mir seinen grauen Grind
und wirft mich fort in den Kot.

The Song of the Drunkard

It wasn't in me. It went out and in.
I wanted to keep it there. The wine held it.
(I don't know anymore what it was.)
Then wine held me this and held me that
until I left everything up to him.
Like a fool.

Now I'm in his game and he scatters
me around with contempt and just today loses me
to this beast, to Death.
When *he* wins a card as filthy as me,
he picks at his gray scabs with it
then tosses it on the dungheap.

Das Lied des Selbstmörders

Also noch einen Augenblick.
Daß sie mir immer wieder den Strick
zerschneiden.
Neulich war ich so gut bereit,
und es war schon ein wenig Ewigkeit
in meinen Eingeweiden.

Halten sie mir den Löffel her,
diesen Löffel Leben.
Nein, ich will und ich will nicht mehr,
laßt mich mich übergeben.

Ich weiß, das Leben ist gar und gut,
und die Welt ist ein voller Topf,
aber mir geht es nicht ins Blut,
mir steigt es nur zu Kopf.

Andere nährt es, mich macht es krank;
begreift, daß man's verschmäht.
Mindestens ein Jahrtausend lang
brauch ich jetzt Diät.

The Song of the Suicide

Well then, another moment.
Again and again they cut
my rope.
The other day I was so ready,
there was a bit of eternity
already in my bowels.

They hold out the spoon to me,
this spoon of life.
No, I want and I want no more,
let me spew myself up.

I know, life is quite good,
and the world is a full pot,
but that doesn't get into my blood,
it only reaches as far as my head.

It nourishes others — it nauseates me;
understand that it can be spurned.
Now, for at least a thousand years,
I need to diet.

19

Das Lied der Witwe

Am Anfang war mir das Leben gut.
Es hielt mich warm, es machte mir Mut.
Daß es das allen Jungen tut,
wie könnt ich das damals wissen.
Ich wußte nicht, was das Leben war –,
auf einmal war es nur Jahr und Jahr,
nicht mehr gut, nicht mehr neu, nicht mehr wunderbar,
wie mitten entzwei gerissen.

Das war nicht seine, nicht meine Schuld;
wir hatten beide nichts als Geduld,
aber der Tod hat keine.
Ich sah ihn kommen (wie schlecht er kam),
und ich schaute ihm zu, wie er nahm und nahm:
es war ja gar nicht das Meine.

Was war denn das Meine; Meines, Mein?
War mir nicht selbst mein Elendsein
nur vom Schicksal geliehn?
Das Schicksal will nicht nur das Glück,
es will die Pein und das Schrein zurück,
und es kauft für alt den Ruin.
Das Schicksal war da und erwarb für ein Nichts

The Song of the Widow

In the beginning, life was good to me.
It kept me warm, it gave me courage.
It does that for all the young,
but how could I have known that then?
I didn't know what life was—,
straightaway, it was just year and year,
no longer good, no longer fresh, drained of wonder,
as if torn right down the middle.

That was not his fault, nor mine;
we both had nothing but patience,
but Death has none.
I saw him coming (how wickedly he came),
and I watched as he took and took:
there was nothing that belonged to me.

Then what was *Mine*; of mine, my own?
Was even my misery
only lent by fate?

Fate wants back not only the happiness,
it wants the howls and the anguish,
then it picks up the ruins for cheap.

jeden Ausdruck meines Gesichts
bis auf die Art zu gehn.
Das war ein täglicher Ausverkauf,
und als ich leer war, gab es mich auf
und ließ mich offen stehn.

Fate was there and, for next to nothing,
got every expression on my face,
down to the mood.
It was a daily selloff
and when I was empty, it gave me up
and left me standing open.

Das Lied des Idioten

Sie hindern mich nicht. Sie lassen mich gehn.
Sie sagen, es könne nichts geschehn.
Wie gut.
Es kann nichts geschehn. Alles kommt und kreist
immerfort um den Heiligen Geist,
um den gewissen Geist (du weißt) –,
wie gut.

Nein, man muß wirklich nicht meinen, es sei
irgend eine Gefahr dabei.
Das ist freilich das Blut.
Das Blut ist das Schwerste. Das Blut ist schwer.
Manchmal glaub ich, ich kann nicht mehr –.
(Wie gut.)

Ah, was ist das für ein schöner Ball;
rot und rund wie ein Überall.
Gut, daß ihr ihn erschuft.
Ob der wohl kommt, wenn man ruft?

Wie sich das alles seltsam benimmt,
ineinandertreibt, auseinanderschwimmt:
freundlich, ein wenig unbestimmt.
Wie gut.

The Song of the Idiot

They don't hinder me. They let me pass.
They say nothing could happen.
How good.
Nothing could happen. Everything comes and circles
constantly around the Holy Ghost,
around that specific ghost (you know) —,
how good.

No, one really must not imagine
there is the least danger in it.
True, there is the blood.
The blood is the hardest. The blood is heavy.
Sometimes I don't think I *can* anymore—.
(How good.)

Oh what a lovely ball that is;
red and round like an everywhere.
Good, that you created it.
It probably comes when you call for it?

How strangely all this behaves,
pushed together, swimming apart:
friendly, a bit blurry.
How good.

Das Lied der Waise

Ich bin Niemand und werde auch Niemand sein.
Jetzt bin ich ja zum Sein noch zu klein;
aber auch später.

Mütter und Väter,
erbarmt euch mein.

Zwar es lohnt nicht des Pflegens Müh:
ich werde doch gemäht.
Mich kann keiner brauchen: jetzt ist es zu früh
und morgen ist es zu spät.

Ich habe nur dieses eine Kleid,
es wird dünn und es verbleicht,
aber es hält eine Ewigkeit
auch noch vor Gott vielleicht.

Ich habe nur dieses bißchen Haar
(immer dasselbe blieb),
das einmal Eines Liebstes war.

Nun hat er nichts mehr lieb.

The Song of the Orphan

I am no one and will also be no one.
Right now I am still too small for being;
but also later.

Mothers and fathers,
have mercy on me.

Admittedly, it's not worth the trouble to raise me:
I'll still be cut down.
No one can use me: now it's too early
and tomorrow it's too late.

I have only this one dress,
it will thin and fade,
but it will last an eternity,
even before God perhaps.

I have only this lock of hair
(it always remains the same)
that once was someone's dearest.

He doesn't love anything anymore.

Das Lied des Zwerges

Meine Seele ist vielleicht grad und gut;
aber mein Herz, mein verbogenes Blut,
alles das, was mir wehe tut,
kann sie nicht aufrecht tragen.
Sie hat keinen Garten, sie hat kein Bett,
sie hängt an meinem scharfen Skelett
mit entsetztem Flügelschlagen.

Aus meinen Händen wird auch nichts mehr.
Wie verkümmert sie sind: sieh her:
zähe hüpfen sie, feucht und schwer,
wie kleine Kröten nach Regen.
Und das Andere an mir ist
abgetragen und alt und trist;
warum zögert Gott, auf den Mist
alles das hinzulegen.

Ob er mir zürnt für mein Gesicht
mit dem mürrischen Munde?
Es war ja so oft bereit, ganz licht
und klar zu werden im Grunde;
aber nichts kam ihm je so dicht
wie die großen Hunde.
Und die Hunde haben das nicht.

The Song of the Dwarf

My soul might be good and straight;
but my heart, my contorted blood,
everything that makes me ache—
it can't keep them upright.
It has no garden, it has no bed,
it clings onto my sharp skeleton
with a terrified beating of wings.

Expect nothing from my hands, either.
How stunted they are: look at them:
they hop tenaciously, damp and heavy,
like little toads after rain.
And the rest of me is
worn out, old, and drab;
what stops God from dumping
this all in the dirt?

Is he angry with me for my face
with its sulky mouth?
It was so often ready to become clear
and bright—in principle;
but nothing ever came as close to it
as big dogs.
And even dogs won't have it.

Das Lied des Aussätzigen

Sieh, ich bin einer, den alles verlassen hat.
Keiner weiß in der Stadt von mir,
Aussatz hat mich befallen.
Und ich schlage mein Klapperwerk,
klopfe mein trauriges Augenmerk
in die Ohren allen,
die nahe vorübergehn.
Und die es hölzern hören, sehn
erst gar nicht her, und was hier geschehn,
wollen sie nicht erfahren.

Soweit der Klang meiner Klapper reicht,
bin ich zuhause; aber vielleicht
machst Du meine Klapper so laut,
daß sich keiner in meine Ferne traut,
der mir jetzt aus der Nähe weicht.
So daß ich sehr lange gehen kann,
ohne Mädchen, Frau oder Mann
oder Kind zu entdecken.
Tiere will ich nicht schrecken.

The Song of the Leper

Look at me, someone forsaken by all.
No one in town knows me,
I'm eaten up with leprosy.
And I beat my clapper,
knocking my cheerless notice
into the ears of all
who pass by.
They hear it woodenly and look
anywhere but here—and what I go through,
they hope never to face.

So far as the sound of my clapper can reach,
I am at home; but if you,
Lord, can make my clapper so loud
that none dare enter my distance
who now shrinks from my nearness,
then I'll be able to go a very long way
with no girl, woman, man,
or child in sight.

I hope not to make animals take flight.

from **NEW POEMS [1907-1908]**

Mädchen-Klage

Diese Neigung, in den Jahren,
da wir alle Kinder waren,
viel allein zu sein, war mild;
andern ging die Zeit im Streite,
und man hatte seine Seite,
seine Nähe, seine Weite,
einen Weg, ein Tier, ein Bild.

Und ich dachte noch, das Leben
hörte niemals auf zu geben,
daß man sich in sich besinnt.
Bin ich in mir nicht im Größten?
Will mich Meines nicht mehr trösten
und verstehen wie als Kind?

Plötzlich bin ich wie verstoßen,
und zu einem Übergroßen
wird mir diese Einsamkeit,
wenn, auf meiner Brüste Hügeln
stehend, mein Gefühl nach Flügeln
oder einem Ende schreit.

Girl's Lament

This inclination, in the years
when we all were children,
to be so often alone, was benign;
others passed their time quarreling,
and one picked one's side,
one's near, one's far,
a path, an animal, an image.

And still I imagined life
would never cease to grant
chances to look in on myself.
Am I not, within myself, exalted?
Will what's mine no longer console
and know me, as in childhood?

Suddenly, it's like I've been cast out,
and this solitude becomes
too vast for me,
when, standing on the hills of my breasts,
my feelings cry out for wings
or for an end.

Eranna an Sappho

O du wilde weite Werferin:
Wie ein Speer bei andern Dingen
lag ich bei den Meinen. Dein Erklingen
warf mich weit. Ich weiß nicht wo ich bin.
Mich kann keiner wiederbringen.

Meine Schwestern denken mich und weben,
und das Haus ist voll vertrauter Schritte.
Ich allein bin fern und fortgegeben,
und ich zittere wie eine Bitte;
denn die schöne Göttin in der Mitte
ihrer Mythen glüht und lebt mein Leben.

Eranna to Sappho

O you fierce far-thrower:
Like a spear alongside unlike things
I lay among my people. Your songs
carried me off. I don't know *where* I am.
No one can bring me back.

My sisters brood on me and weave,
and the house is full of familiar footsteps.
I alone am distant, a disciple,
and I tremble in entreaty;
because the beautiful goddess glows
from the heart of her myths and lives my life.

Sappho an Eranna

Unruh will ich über dich bringen,
schwingen will ich dich, umrankter Stab.
Wie das Sterben will ich dich durchdringen
und dich weitergeben wie das Grab
an das Alles: allen diesen Dingen.

Sappho to Eranna

I want to immerse you in unrest,
I want to shake you, entangled staff.
I want to pierce through you like dying
and, like the grave, hand you over
to Everything: all these things.

Pietà

So seh ich, Jesus, deine Füße wieder,
die damals eines Jünglings Füße waren,
da ich sie bang entkleidete und wusch;
wie standen sie verwirrt in meinen Haaren
und wie ein weißes Wild im Dornenbusch.

So seh ich deine niegeliebten Glieder
zum erstenmal in dieser Liebesnacht.
Wir legten uns noch nie zusammen nieder,
und nun wird nur bewundert und gewacht.

Doch, siehe, deine Hände sind zerrissen –:
Geliebter, nicht von mir, von meinen Bissen.
Dein Herz steht offen und man kann hinein:
das hätte dürfen nur mein Eingang sein.

Nun bist du müde, und dein müder Mund
hat keine Lust zu meinem wehen Munde –.
O Jesus, Jesus, wann war unsre Stunde?
Wie gehn wir beide wunderlich zugrund.

Pietà

So, Jesus, I see your feet once again.
You had a young man's feet back then
which I anxiously unshod and washed:
how they tangled in my hair
like white deer in thorny brush.

So I see your never-loved limbs
for the first time on this night of love.
We never got to lie together,
now I can only admire and keep watch.

But look, your hands are torn—:
Beloved, not by me, not from my bite.
Your heart stands open and anyone can enter:
It should have been my entrance alone.

Now you are tired and your weary lips
have no appetite for my aching mouth—.
O Jesus, Jesus, when was our hour?
How strangely we both perish.

Der Gefangene

I.

Meine Hand hat nur noch eine
Gebärde, mit der sie verscheucht;
auf die alten Steine
fällt es aus Felsen feucht.

Ich höre nur dieses Klopfen
und mein Herz hält Schritt
mit dem Gehen der Tropfen
und vergeht damit.
Tropften sie doch schneller,
käme doch wieder ein Tier.
Irgendwo war es heller –.
Aber was wissen wir.

The Prisoner

I.

My hand has only one
gesture — I frighten them off with it;
Onto ancient stones,
drops fall from dank rocks above.

I hear only this rhythm
and my heart keeps pace
with the sounding of the drops
and vanishes with them.
If they'd only drip faster,
an animal might come again.
Somewhere it was brighter —.
But what do we know.

II.

Denk dir, das was jetzt Himmel ist und Wind,

Luft deinem Mund und deinem Auge Helle,

das würde Stein bis um die kleine Stelle

an der dein Herz und deine Hände sind.

Und was jetzt in dir morgen heißt und: dann

und: späterhin und nächstes Jahr und weiter –

das würde wund in dir und voller Eiter

und schwäre nur und bräche nicht mehr an.

Und das was war, das wäre irre und

raste in dir herum, den lieben Mund

der niemals lachte, schäumend von Gelächter.

Und das was Gott war, wäre nur dein Wächter

und stopfte boshaft in das letzte Loch

ein schmutziges Auge. Und du lebtest doch.

II.

Imagine that what is now sky and wind,
air for your mouth and light for your eyes,
became stone up to the small place
where your heart and hands are.

And what you now call *tomorrow* and: *then*
and: *later on* and *next year* and onward —
became a wound full of pus
that only festered and never broke open.

And that which was would go insane and
rave around inside you; your dear mouth
that never laughed, frothing with laughter.

And what had been God would just be your warder
and spitefully shove a filthy eye
into every last hole; and yet you *lived*.

Leichen-Wäsche

Sie hatten sich an ihn gewöhnt. Doch als
die Küchenlampe kam und unruhig brannte
im dunkeln Luftzug, war der Unbekannte
ganz unbekannt. Sie wuschen seinen Hals,

und da sie nichts von seinem Schicksal wußten,
so logen sie ein anderes zusamm,
fortwährend waschend. Eine mußte husten
und ließ solang den schweren Essigschwamm

auf dem Gesicht. Da gab es eine Pause
auch für die zweite. Aus der harten Bürste
klopften die Tropfen; während seine grause
gekrampfte Hand dem ganzen Hause
beweisen wollte, daß ihn nicht mehr dürste.

Und er bewies. Sie nahmen wie betreten
eiliger jetzt mit einem kurzen Huster
die Arbeit auf, so daß an den Tapeten
ihr krummer Schatten in dem stummen Muster

sich wand und wälzte wie in einem Netze,
bis daß die Waschenden zu Ende kamen.
Die Nacht im vorhanglosen Fensterrahmen

Corpse Washing

They had grown used to him. Even so, as
the kitchen lamp entered and burned fitfully
in the dark draft, this unknown one was still
wholly unknown. They washed his neck,

and because they knew nothing of his fate,
they invented one for him together,
washing all the while. One had to cough
and, as she did, left the heavy vinegar-sponge

on his face. Then the other also paused to rest.
Drop after drop fell from the hard brush;
meanwhile, his horrible cramped hand
wanted to prove to the whole house
that he was no longer thirsty.

And it was proven. With a short cough,
as if embarrassed, they took up their work
more urgently, so that their crooked shadows
twined and rolled on the wallpaper's

mute pattern as though in a net,
until the washing came to an end.
The night in the curtainless windows

war rücksichtslos. Und einer ohne Namen
lag bar und reinlich da und gab Gesetze.

was heedless. And the one with no name
lay there bare and clean, giving orders.

About the author

Rainer Maria Rilke was born in Prague in 1875 and died of leukemia in Switzerland in 1926. Never in doubt about his vocation as poet, his work was the product of a tireless growth—work which may accurately be seen as a bridge leading from *fin de siècle* literature into Modernism.

About the translator

Kristofor Minta is a writer and translator. Twice a finalist in the National Poetry Series, he is a graduate of Syracuse University's MFA program. His translations (with Herbert Pföstl) of Hans Jürgen von der Wense have been published as *A Shelter for Bells* by Epidote Press.

SUBLUNARY

EDITIONS

Sublunary Editions is a small, independent press based in Seattle, Washington. It publishes short books of innovative writing from a worldwide cadre of authors, past and present. Subscriptions are available at: subeds.com/subscribe

Lamplight Editions is a small press based in the Pacific Northwest, occasionally publishing poetry and fiction in translation.